# A Lot Can Happen...

## When a girl goes to the west

Dr Chitrangada Loves

BookLeaf Publishing

India | USA | UK

Made with ❤ on the BookLeaf Publishing Platform
www.bookleafpub.in
www.bookleafpub.com

# Dedication

*...Because time can be squeezed and stretched
but never reversed,
let this be an account of how past struggled to
make future triumph without the present knowing!*

# Preface

*Life can be painless, provided that there is sufficient
peacefulness
for a dozen or so rituals to be repeated simply endlessly.
Time and space abound by the talks that play charade
with the minds of us kids satirically.
Bright days, funny nights, sleepless beds to gutful sights.
The Utopia was coming alive. The dance of the angles
killed the demon's by their vibe.
May be...
Who knows for sure; aren't we just a glitch in the
universe after all!*

*Hence, I only wish to write about the philosophy of my
time lived
or about the enlightenment I learn to seek.
This quick letter is just about my momentary existence.
The existence probably we all flip from and towards,
but hardly care to catch as a stream of consciousness.*

*But today, I decided to retrospect over my current being
and look back
on those days of melancholy, overexcitement, sloth filled
days, and also the state of just being still,
unmanipulated by thoughts.*

*To gather meaning from another is lazy living but that is
how you function
when your engine is not oiled for adventure.
Let this collection of intended wordplay powered by the
experience of a few decades
find you as a happy reader paving your own path on a
road that wants wear.
I sincerely hope you relate. I wish to channelize and
connect with you,
I really do!*

# Acknowledgements

*Nature is the best teacher if you are paying attention.*
*All encompassing nature, within and without.*
*A mother is a strong force of nature.*
*One you will forever learn from,*
*present or gone.*

# 1. Mad woman

*Before the madness kicks in,*
*I lie here in solitude of my own nerves.*
*They play humor with me to bring those vivacious*
*rather painful mind palace to my notice again.*
*My body runs in chills which the incoming breeze brings*
*in.*

*She felt like that harsh dry leaf*
*that kills itself with your gentle touch.*
*Although my liking for it makes me bias towards it,*
*telling the world that*
*the leaf was soothed by her cold*
*in reciprocation of her heat earlier today.*

*Dead was the water, married to its shallowness*
*but the duck was the free philosopher*
*swimming it's notes down.*
*Grey was the new golden in the town which obliged*
*who ever saw it,*
*to call it dead beautiful.*

*The selenophiles were still sleeping,*
*while their moon was trotting to being crescent again*
*with no star audience to applaud for her*
*but the mad woman that still didn't kick in.*

I

# 2. She is the creator

*The cycle of life begins with the desire of our selfish genes*
*to never stop exploring, moving towards evolutionary complexities,*
*forever dwelling in the idea of immortality.*


*Hence you and I were born.*
*I wear your nose and lips and see the world through my eyes*
*so that I can be your new eyes.*
*I offer my ears to you as you tell me how the world was,*
*so my mind can be prepared on modes of how to be.*
*You are protecting me now, so I can protect you then.*
*It's a trade of life,*
*You better get your honeys' worth*


*Blood is thicker than water, yes.*
*But then blood of the covenant is thicker than the water of the womb,*

family you make is more meaningful of your identity
than the family you come from.


I am your choices and nurture imparted.
My life has been your giving, my receiving,
a blessing and a learning.
A third of my life through, I see similarities in me from
you
They comfort and scare me,
so I shall prepare to face the wrath of time if history
repeats.
Anticipation of an event may give rise to one;
Denial of knowledge can curtain the wrath of mind,


In shadows cast by choices made, I walk the tightrope of
fate,
Each step a dance between the past and the future I must
navigate.
Glimmers of hope flicker in the twilight, whispering
softly to my soul,
From the pieces of our stories, a new narrative can be a
whole.

# 3. Home on my back

*Long gone were our cradle wheels, turned and twisted
to fit back into the treasure box
which none would find for decades.*

*My Bunny bag and orange pacifier are long rust
to the separation we suffered when five.
Those 10 dollar yearly book pile was long bartered for
1000 paise rag
None of them competed with my cognitive spaces for
residence anymore,
so why does the nerve potential spike, losing its
threshold to the tendencies
I once called home.
We all have them. Tendencies!
Neither are mine better than yours nor yours bigger than
mine.
Still there are these innocent little tendencies
we carry as we grow up,
as every year passes,
even after intervals of seven years, they stay,*

*with none of your body cell recognizing the other, they*
*still crave.*

*I am the turtle able to live simply anywhere,*
*even underwater for short periods, with my home on my*
*back.*
*And in some corner there,*
*I still hide my tendencies.*

# 4. Foreign Breath

*There will come a point, a phase, in the journey*
*where your breath will be foreign...*
*These down days will make you feel alien in your skin*
*Existence will scream to find the joy of life and soon*
*will spiral into the womb of black holes*
*Sadness that stays long enough to become nothingness*
*Don't mind it too much*
*It's all part of the journey*
*Don't embrace it close to the heart,*
*like gold or flowers*
*This too shall leave you like the cloud of a windy land*

*Time*
*Be patient with time, and your spirit*
*Those days are for nurturing self with soul hugs*
*and a nice warm tea in bed*
*An old melody that soothes the nerves*
*Or a walk in the busy street to slow the drums*

*Believe in the Sun to shine through those clouds*

*Believe in the land to bring you some warmth*
*Smile equally on the good and bad you endured*
*It is this fair response to duality that will bring sanity*
*and soon the foreign breath will accept the land*

*Left home when I was twelve, my mind was starting to*
*swell*
*Loud noises hit my aquarium, silence became it's*
*requiem*
*Missing my home, peeping through drones*
*Stepping on two boats got me sick*
*Leaving with two notes got me rich*

# 5. Lost in the way

*Is it okay to not be fixed, but be confused,
to not have sides, to be flexible to changing times
or waves of mood to be fragile, to being uncoordinated,
to deflect a changing tribe.
To be accommodating to various moves of emotions.
Write on the wall whichever way I want;
Leaving me subjective, unpredictable
and yet somewhere I feel this is
not the way to live.
One must know what they want, what to do and how to
do it.*

*To know where to go but not reach, is getting lost
But to not know where to go, is a time for exploration
In my experience, getting lost in an explorative
expedition
is the best kind of lost
Cause only then finding the way to the horizon,
brings peace like home*

*Amidst the chaos, I learn to breathe,*
*Treading paths unseen, where the heart believes.*
*Each turn, a lesson; every stumble, a dance,*
*In the wild embrace of fate, I find my chance.*

*So let me wander, let me stray,*
*In the unpredictable night, I'll shape my day.*
*With every layer shed, I grow more whole,*
*In the art of becoming, I'm finding my soul.*

# 6. Choose the chaos

*This life has been given a time*
*What would you do? Seek god or seek evil*
*Or be stuck in the middle of both*
*Form or destroy, or be stagnant.*
*Lay around, waste time or use it*
*Maybe your wounds or everything around you, all stink,*
*nothing interests you*
*What then?*
*Seek Truth!*
*But where do you find it? Whom do you follow?*
*Who do you lead? What do you trust?*

*Balance is an opposite of crazy*
*Balance is the key to a sane life*
*Crazy leads to extremes*
*Maybe extreme is for you*
*Or maybe it will kill you*
*Choice is yours*
*Chaos or calm...*
*Time teaches you, grows you*

*Destroys you, finishes you*
*Beliefs make you, works for you*
*Or against*
*Either way it will stay with you*
*Do what you believe in*
*Cause the other might kill you*
*Your surrounding influences you*
*Choose your set & setting*
*Calm is only calm from far*
*Get close, touch it, it burns...*

*So choose your fire, let it ignite,*
*Flickering shadows dance in the night.*
*Every heartbeat a chance to decide,*
*In the chaos, find where you hide.*
*Will you stand firm, or will you sway?*
*In the battle of thoughts, who will you play?*
*Life's fragile thread, both strength and tether,*
*In this fleeting moment, we search for forever.*

# 7. Look within

*We became cripplingly specialized as halves of that genius,*
*the most important individual of our lives, but we never named it.*
*It died as quickly as we were parted, and was reborn the moment we got together again.*

*Your mind divides, the senses categorize;*
*the oneness of existence into parts,*
*"me and other", "this and that", subject and object.*
*Like a prism, one existence refracts into a million*
*Veil of mind punishes the body and spirit*
*with a dangerous realm of illusion.*
*bringing chaos in harmony of your universe.*

*However, there is a place in the unfolding of understanding,*
*a perspective for interpretation of their duality.*

*For the mind doesn't really divide existence.*

*It only appears so.*
*There is nothing illusory about the world.*
*It is the separation between the Existence of the world*
*from the seat of Consciousness, that is illusory*
*This illusion of a separate and independent existence is*
*created through mind and senses.*
*It is the creativity of Consciousness,*
*through the faculties of mind and senses,*
*which refracts Oneness into a dance of apparent*
*multiplicity.*
*Time is the first language of the mind.*
*Space is the first language of the senses.*
*Remove time and space from experience*
*that is, remove name and form*
*and we are left with the Oneness of Consciousness/*
*Existence.*

*We are left with timeless, spaceless presence, with*
*"Being".*
*Being shines in the self as consciousness and in the*
*world as existence.*

# 8. Anger

*Some feeling*
*When you want to resist opposition and prove yourself*
*Who is watching you, no clue*
*who cares even, only you*
*a survival carnal feeling*
*Its defensive*
*Wants to protect self from damage,*
*Self preservation mode*
*Go silent*
*Guard your walls*
*Don't let anyone in*
*Well this will make you a good watchman*
*But, Who likes the watchman?*

*Anger is useful I say.*
*Use it productively!*
*Let it fuel you with purpose*
*Its helpful to prove your worth*
*Maybe just in your own eyes...*

*As shadows loom and whispers creep,*
*Building fortresses—no time for sleep.*
*A fortress made of fears and doubts,*
*Yet outside, the world is what life is about*

*Break the chains of that watchman's gaze,*
*And step into the sun*
*Embrace the rays.*

# 10. Tunnel Vision

*I will wake up and swing my life with zest,*
*tomorrow is a new day*
*I repeat to myself.*
*Swimming in shallow sleep of horrendous tastes,*
*I will close my eyes further*
*to avoid the actual case.*
*Mornings aren't as yellow*
*as they seem for all,*
*somedays blue was the rhythm for me to crawl.*
*Resilience was what I taught myself for dawn,*
*While slipping back to bipolarity for sun down.*
*This won't happen tomorrow*
*I repeat to myself,*
*tomorrow I will wake up and swing my life with zest.*

*You are what you tell your head everyday*
*from the dawn of your glittery eyes*
*to the dusk of your golden ways*

# 10. Helicopter Perspective

*A great mind is like the canoe,*
*of which the "Will" is the paddle.*
*The reality that we seem to have created for ourselves*
*is a living illusion of the mind.*

*My Will makes me breathe ,stop it, live or die.*
*So will you dare to give into your Will?*
*Or will you dare to break your paddle and stay still in*
*your canoe forever?*

*I will come from the east*
*when the mist pulls me like the gravity*
*I will pull you out into my arms*
*And you could lie there for infinity*

*Let the folds of your greased minds*
*close forever into that dried heap of grey*
*that brought no mercy to your sane.*

*Step out in the darkness, with your eyes closed,*
*Detach to the meaning of a lost tale.*
*The Sun will rise again, with your eyes now open*
*the light will change the game.*

*The moon got bloated with high words,*
*it drowned in the nothingness of the sky.*
*Ride the helicopter away from the damaged site*
*Only to see the mind gain the wise sight*

# 11. Slow down

*In circles we stood with hope stretching our spine*
*with haste in our right palm and curiosity in our left.*
*10 entities,10 energies and with those 1000 beats being*
*played*
*those 10,000 thoughts raced.*

*When you shelter a thought, let your body make a drink*
*of it*
*Slowly and steadily allow her to fall in love with*
*Haste they say is the Devil's foreplay*
*Tomorrow you may have questions to answer*
*when you turn gray*

*When you haste to eat their cake*
*You live a life that is fake*
*Why armor the duality with hypocrisy*
*When sooner or later you will be drowning in a sludge*
*of hay*
*Guilt, the tug that keeps tugging at your will*

*Its sits in your heart like the morning dew sits on the*
*window sill*
*So when you shelter a thought, let your body make a*
*drink of it*
*Slowly and steadily allow her to fall in love with*
*If tomorrow you leave the thought for another*
*Make love harder this time till you see the dawn of*
*another*

*Tomorrow when you have questions to answer*
*Let your body take a drink and sip*

# 12. What you know, you know

*To the mother, whose hands are like the slender leaf*
*looking through the wildest caves,*
*for sunshine for that flower, that child of hers;*
*For whom even if her hands have to*
*bruise and sow,*
*they will.*
*For whom even if her hands have to*
*bleed when they demand to stay still,*
*they will.*
*Then she was old*

*Now she is more,*
*a terrible walker, way worse in her handlings,*
*shiver could be her new name.*
*She still blesses you, bless her flower,*
*bless that child of hers with those trembling palms*
*which she won't raise for a glass.*

*But she surely would offer you some, a glass, eine tasse
tee,
oh that sweet old woman, her heart would order her
spine to get up
from that ever lasting heavy gravity on to those feet
which may now have forgotten what they once did.*

*For some people life can be such a crushing event,
when gravity turns mean.*

# 13. What you know, you don't know

*You gave birth to my melody,*
*the rhythm of which echoed into the corner slits of even*
*are neighbour's door.*

*Pure, a bliss,*
*this soul I carry, carries a thousand faces,*
*anonymous, blurred, unknown whom I wanna kiss.*

*You were that corner slit, whom I often visited*
*in days when thousand never existed and one was all I*
*knew about.*

*You are weak now and I am angry*
*You were my master and I was your beat*
*While now, how shall this beat-beat!*

*You cry, whine, swirl like a baby*
*when I need you to get up and run miles with me.*
*You wouldn't. You can maybe; but you will disagree.*

*You call out for me, I feel terrified.*
*Don't talk of leaving,*
*I feel numb and petrified.*
*Dumb! I have acquired no remedy for the soul*
*that could burn fire into cold ash in seconds.*
*I find no instrument for that master, who made this beat.*

# 14. The only way out is, through

*Does the unknown scare you*
*Or does the known petrify you*
*Do you wait for serendipity to happen*
*But run for isolation when it does*
*Your teeth feel sour*
*And so does your chapped neck*
*You bite your lips*
*And wait endlessly for love*

*You are half the sky you can be*
*And more than the feet that keep you back*
*May you go beautiful again*
*Fierce be your core*
*Halo be your protector*
*And your mind - body - soul be one again like before*
*But just new to endure*

# 15. The First Love

*With the first cry, her supple hands held mine*
*It is a bond set in the books before my birth*

*A bond where she invested a river of emotions and*
*thoughts*
*even before I learned to drink a drop*
*It started with a desire to hold, to kiss and feed,*
*to share, to show and lead*

*It had undertones of unspoken shadows that she*
*wouldn't admit,*
*to avoid cracking the ego that flaunts perfection*
*but there was the whole light and darkness to this desire*
*that will soon learn to evolve.*

*They say "the darkness holds more truth than the light*
*can ever see"*
*Such is the wisdom of saints, to embrace the shadows of*
*one's light,*
*accept reality as a whorl*

*that shall never be escaped; only endured, lived and
experienced.*

*Her shadows forecasted her expectations,
a desire for power, her pain, her tears, left on seen.
The pressure of the unknown, unseen forces that
brought chaos into her being,
now grew in heron their own timeline
whilst she waited in agony,
or hope by the river of her emotions.*

# 16. When the world collapses

What started as one drag,
Caused replay in frustrating search of an experienced
high
That armchair was no more a seat but a throne
for silencing wobbling of their eyes


Blues once again were the poetry of the clock
while chords came to life more than the lubb sound
Reality was more than real and monotony never more
meaningful
My body wanted shakes
while my mind wanted to graph it using all the shades
It was a paradox
It felt all so real and all so still at the same


Like the laws of science decided to take a break,
bring all my knowledge to doubt
I was lying there on the sheets reading my feelings,
echoing my emotions, unreasoning my thoughts,

*speaking my nerves.*

*I won't tell you what I feel. For you won't believe me for*
*now*
*I told the overwhelmed him who was helpless but to*
*witness it all*
*Lying with me, standing with me, picking me in his*
*arms,*
*he was there but I wasn't or maybe*
*My closed eyes had become my gateway to trance*
*My body was there, turning and gliding tongues*
*together,*
*dancing over dry tunes but my mind was watching a*
*movie,*
*my soul loitering in the celestial, detouring around the*
*cosmic truths.*

# 17. Hello from the other side!

*Can I knock on hollow drums and not expect to receive a*
*sound?*
*Can I hit my hand on a hard rock and not feel the brunt*
*of it all?*
*Would it be okay if all my love was crushed,*
*and I refuse to not spit back?*
*Because how else do you deal with all the hurt!*

*People who act like sponges for others sob,*
*expect love in return.*
*But the world doesn't guarantee it's faithfulness to you.*

*So why expect!; Well, why do it at all?*
*A soaking sponge doesn't guarantee love back.*
*Maybe you get all the love from the world when*
*you acclaim it as rightfully yours.*
*"I am loving in my being".*

*To soak ones sob means to reduce the loving vibrations*
*of your being*
*with sadness*
*but to love your being as I love my being*
*means to reduce your sob without trying to soak it.*
*Now understand, there's no guarantee that hurt won't*
*find its way back*
*or that love will*
*but being loving in my act is how*
*I would call myself from the other side.*

# 18. Sun & Moon

*The world runs a cyclical manner,*
*with opportunities for variations,*
*but always around the same theme.*
*Everyday, the sun rises, the moon rises, and both set.*
*The moon's intensity varies more or less.*
*Some days, the wind blows and brings a foreign quest.*

*Everyday, the body rises and falls, and the mind accepts*
*the forces*
*and flows like a river or a flash,*
*causing a forest fire.*

*The journey is running, but we are evolving in our ways.*
*accepting the polarities but calm at the centre,*
*a balancing act, everyday*

*Feeding the right wolf of health, joy, freedom, love &*
*togetherness,*
*starving the wolf of negativity that persists after the*
*lesson is learnt.*

*Instead of narrowing in on the lesson, concentrate on the
experience, the conclusion, and iterate
around the action to be domino in reality to establish
new order.*


*Hold the sacred space of calm and order where wisdom
is persistent and energies are whole
This space is the home, absolute home.
Desire authentically, set intention and actions in place.
Don't allow the noise of self-judgment and judgment of
others
to affect what holds true of your path.
Inform and vocalise and then respect the boundaries set.
Boundaries to protect the sacred home of self and of
others too.*


*Protect and secure the fort, the castle inside the fort,
and hold the sacred temple that lies within.
Keep family close with love, care, support, and
vulnerability
keep the heart open
Let's raise our vibrations together.*

# 19. Gratitude & Surrender

*The desire is to unite and be one with the other*
*Only then, the love will flourish like a burning sun.*
*The union of two bodies and two minds to bring forth*
*magic,*
*demands love.*
*Love is to take another and make it a part of yourself*
*It all starts with one feeling,*
*the feeling of gratefulness, thankfulness.*

*The feeling of gratitude for all that you experience,*
*unites you to the external.*
*It dissolves the boundaries created by the intellect*
*or the ego.*
*You let the outside be a pleasant experience,*
*opening up the dynamic flow between*
*your inner and outer world.*
*That's the beginning of wisdom.*

*Embody the feeling,*
*This will bring forth a lot of happiness and peace.*

*Security will grow in our being*
*The need of the hardwired survival instincts will mellow*
*down,*
*in that our unnecessary attachments cease*
*we begin to understand the fiction better.*


*Then all there is, is surrender.*
*Surrender to all that union brings.*
*The good, the bad, the mundane.*
*Become fully involved in the process with the fellow of*
*entanglement.*
*Only in absolute surrender we will experience union*
*that will have the power to make us whole,*
*an absolute.*
*Only in absolute surrender can divine reside,*
*only than can our soul's divine find*
*absoluteness, undying and almighty source of energy.*

# 20. Grow

*It doesn't have to be perfect,*
*Trust yourself.*
*Can you hear the the time talking to you,*
*whispering with its gentle yet forceful twists against the*
*wind?*
*Hear! It says something, it calls for you.*

*The heavy heart when you look back in reminiscence*
*shall get worse, but I shall be optimistic and remind you,*
*o' child! This too shall pass!*

*I know you are staying,*
*just getting comfortable in this broken chair of yours.*
*pretty, yet broken and I would have to ask you to get up,*
*o' child it's now that the time demands you to grow up!*
*I am moving, trying to lift my spine,*
*pivoting that pelvis to raise my anteriors and reach out*
*for myself.*

*My mother once narrated a legend against a story of*
*nature,*
*she hinted me to become that Eagle who would break his*
*beak,*
*his paws, cut through his wings,*
*endure the pain for a whole 150 days to grow.*
*Grow from that shallow bird and evolve into the one*
*which soars high,*
*beyond the chains of his own mediocrity.*
*Mother! I am trying to be that Eagle.*
*Trust me I want to.*
*It's patience against Time now. And time is pain!*

# 21. Here & Now

*Take no thought for t'morrow*
*for t'morrow shall take thought for the things of itself.*

*Life is a blessing, breath is life.*
*Feel it all softly. Slow down.*
*Take every second in, don't let them rush you.*

*Stay connected to loving feminine*
*Closely obsessed in thoughts of her lover running*
*autopilot*
*an intense dedicated tunnel visioned lover*
*That's all is here, all that to do now.*

*Time, routine, self, non-self all lost meaning*
*in the everyday since all waking life is spent*
*connected to her lover, in presence or absence!*

*The feminine needs a stable masculine home to breath*
*and sigh into.*
*Let her thicken her blood and size up her breasts.*

*Feel the body talking and look at herself through the*
*eyes of her lover,*
*sexy and dandy, authentic and beautiful, adored and*
*loved.*
*It brings wholesome peace.*

*He brings a desire to step into a new future.*
*The strength is mine to uphold and walk the path,*
*honoring us and others behind; to build and to*
*do justice to the gifts of nature within,*
*play the blessings to the best use.*

*The ones who gave birth are now dry.*
*To water them with our vital strength.*
*Be prudent! Act wise.*
*Bring in and spread out the goodness.*
*...with good health upon us*

# 22. Union

*Touch ground*
*So you see, we flesh skinned spirits always have to come*
*back around*
*to these states of aligning our plan of actions into a new*
*loop of being*
*We constantly need to access the equilibrium and*
*implement the change*
*There is no peace. We find it. We lose it. We find it again.*

*Humanity should live only in a sense which*
*carries meaning and is full of pleasantness.*
*The sadness inflicted roots from meaningless superficial*
*conduct from the same society on itself, other life forms*
*and nature.*
*To restore the balance, this unhealthy sentient manure of*
*beings shall be abolished,*
*one plus all shall live and thrive only in love, health,*
*peace, abundance,*
*compassion, empathy, contribution, goodness.*

*Awareness of purpose drives us everyday, keeps us*
*happy*
*the actions then happen from a place of higher self.*


*Life has a funny way of dealing cards to us,*
*these packs of crayons we go possessive for and keep*
*looking for*
*a canvas to colour on.*
*You might have an eight-pack or a sixteen-pack one,*
*you might be eyeing your neighbour's pack to pull, have*
*no clue to do with yours;*
*but the hope is you would make the best canvas you can*
*and make the best with your crayons.*

www.ingramcontent.com/pod-product-compliance
Lightning Source LLC
LaVergne TN
LVHW021300200726

843509LV00012B/1733